Slam Dunk for Mark

Written by
Rob Waring and **Maurice Jamall**

Before You Read

be sick (not well)

doctor

to cook

finals

to throw

grandma → grandmother

basketball team

cup

vegetable soup

dinner

7:00 PM

busy

In the story

Mark

Mark's grandmother

Anthony

"Give me the ball, Mark!" shouts Anthony.
Today is a big basketball game. Bayview High School
is playing Newtown High School.
Both teams are very good. Newtown High is winning.
Mark and Anthony play for Bayview High. Mark is
Bayview's star player.

The game is very exciting. There is only a little more time. The score is 75 points to Newtown High, and 74 points to Bayview High.

The Newtown player throws the ball, but Mark stops it. Bayview High has one more minute to win the game. . .

Mark has the ball now. He goes around one player, and another.
He jumps and . . . it's a slam dunk! Two points for Bayview!
Bayview High wins the game!
Bayview High can go to the finals tomorrow afternoon.
"Bayview! Bayview! Bayview!" shout the Bayview High students.

"Great play, Mark!" says Anthony.
The basketball team is very happy with Mark.
"Great job, Mark!" says his team.
"Thanks! Good game everybody!" says Mark.
"Good game, everybody. We'll win the cup tomorrow!" he says.

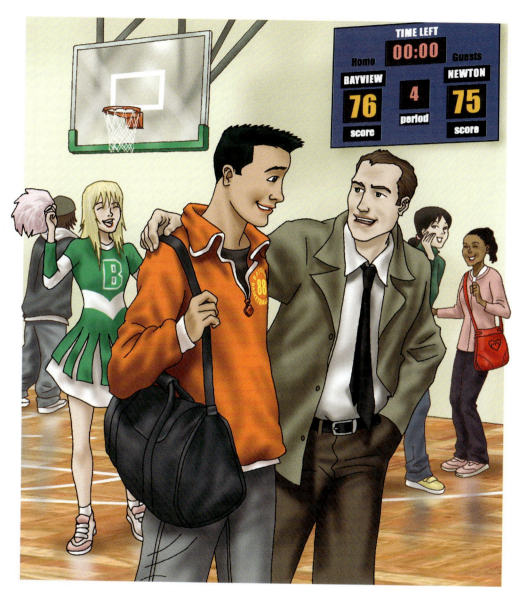

Mark's teacher, Mr. Harris, says, "Good job, Mark, and good luck in tomorrow's game. With you on the team, we'll win the cup again!"

"Thanks, Mr. Harris. Yes, we'll win," says Mark. "We have a good team. We'll win!"

Mark gets home. He usually gets home at 6 o'clock, but today his grandmother is sick again. It's now 4 o'clock that afternoon.

"I'm home, Grandma," he says.

Mark lives with his grandmother. He loves her very much. He has no mother and no father. His grandmother is very old, and sometimes she is not well.

"Grandma," he says. "Are you okay?"

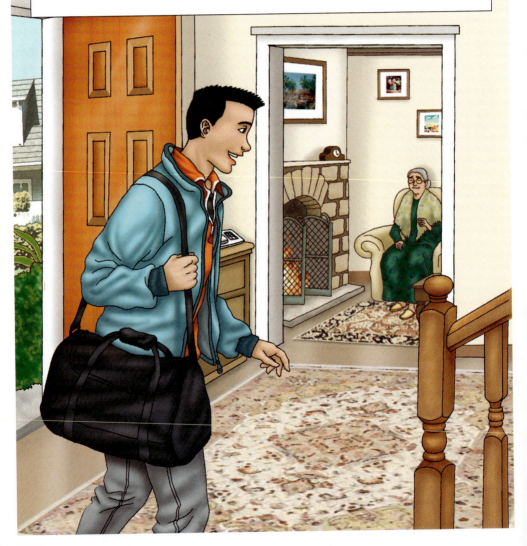

"Hello, Mark." she says. "No, I'm sick again. But tell me about your basketball game. Is your team playing in the finals, Mark?" she asks.

"Yes, we are," he replies. "We're in the finals now. The game is tomorrow afternoon."

His grandmother says, "The finals? Really? That's great, Mark." She is very happy for Mark. She smiles at him.

Mark likes to make dinner for his grandmother.
He asks, "What do you want for dinner, Grandma?"
"Let's have a nice vegetable soup," she says.
Mark says, "That's a good idea. Okay, I'll make that."
She says, "Thank you, Mark. You're very good to me."
"You wait there, Grandma," he says.

Mark gets dinner ready. He likes cooking.
He often cooks for his grandmother. And he always cooks when his grandmother is sick.
He makes vegetable soup, a salad, and many other things.
Mark is a very good cook.
"Grandma, dinner's ready," he says.

Mark looks at his grandmother. He is worried about her.
"Let's go to the doctor tomorrow after school," he says.
She says, "Thank you, Mark. But you have a basketball game
tomorrow. I want you to play. You never miss a game."
"I know, Grandma. But I'm not worried about the game," he
says. "I'm worried about you. I'll take you to the doctor's."

At school the next morning, Anthony says to Mark, "We'll win this afternoon, Mark. With you on the team, we'll win the cup." He is very excited.

"I can't play this afternoon," says Mark.

Anthony is really surprised. "What? You can't play! Why?"

"I'm busy this afternoon," says Mark.

"Busy?" says Anthony. "Busy! But, you're never too busy for basketball! And it's the finals."

"I'm sorry, I can't play," says Mark.

Everybody in school is angry with Mark. He always plays in the finals, but he will not play that afternoon. They want the school to win the cup.

They do not know about his sick grandmother. Mark does not want to tell them about her.

"He's too busy," says Anthony to his friend, Mike.

"Listen, I *am* busy this afternoon. I'm sorry," Mark says.

But nobody listens to Mark. They all want him to play. They do not understand him.

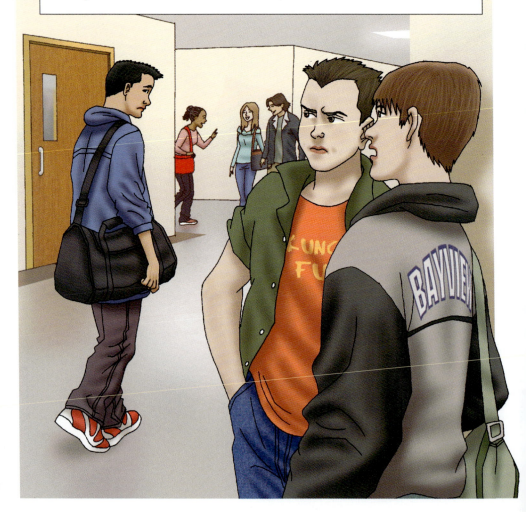

At lunchtime, Mark wants to sit with his friend, Gemma.
He goes to Gemma's table.
"You can't sit here!" she says to Mark.
"Excuse me?" says Mark. "Why?"
"Only my *friends* can sit here," Gemma says. "And *you* are not my friend."
Nobody wants to sit with Mark. Nobody wants to eat with him. They are angry. They want him to play. Mark is very sad.

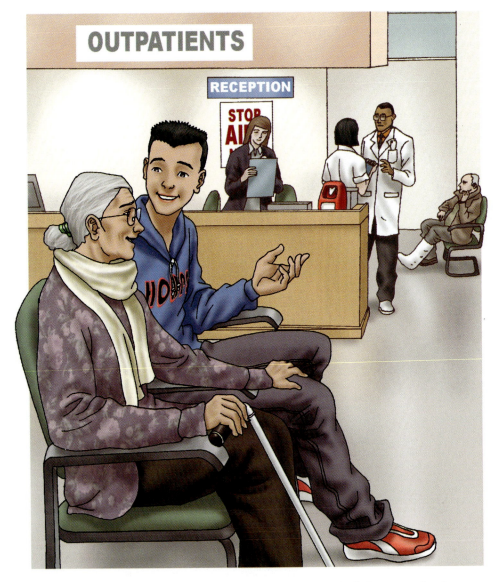

Later that afternoon is the big game. But Mark is not playing basketball. He is with his grandmother at the doctor's.

"Thank you for coming with me, Mark," says his grandmother.

"That's okay, Grandma," he says. "I want to be here. You'll be well soon. You're very important to me. And basketball is only a game."

"Sometimes, people don't understand that," he says.

Kung Fu Kid

Written by
Rob Waring and **Maurice Jamall**

to bow

to fight

to hit

to jump

to kick

to laugh

to move

arm

face

leg

hurt

small

small

tall

tall

In the story

Adib

Ray

Mike

Scott

Kung Fu
teacher

"Are you new?" a boy asks Adib.
Adib is at the kung fu class. It is his first day in the class. There are many people there. They are waiting for the teacher.
"Yes, I am," Adib says. "I'm Adib."
"Hi, I'm Ray," the boy says.

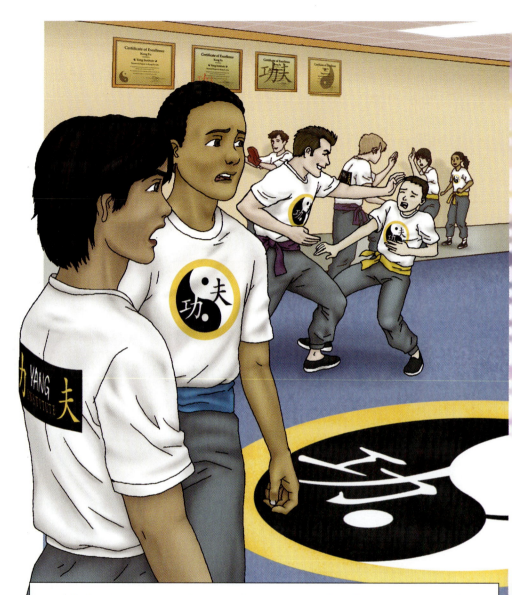

Adib looks at the other students. Some big boys are fighting some small boys.

Ray talks to Adib about one of the boys. "That's Mike Henson," says Ray. "He's very good at kung fu."

"Yes, but the boy is too small," says Adib. "He will get hurt."

"Yes, I know," says Ray. "Mike likes to hurt smaller boys."

Adib is getting ready for class. He is watching another boy.
"Who's that?" Adib asks Ray.
"Scott Nash," says Ray. "He's very good, but he likes to hit people, too."
"I can see," says Adib. The small boy is hurt.

"Stop that!" Adib says to Scott. "Stop!"
Scott stops fighting with the boy. "Why? Who are you?" asks Scott.
"I'm Adib Murad," he says. "That boy can't fight you. You are bigger than he is. You'll hurt him."
"Then you come here and fight me," says Scott. "Come on!"
"Not now," says Adib. "The teacher's here."

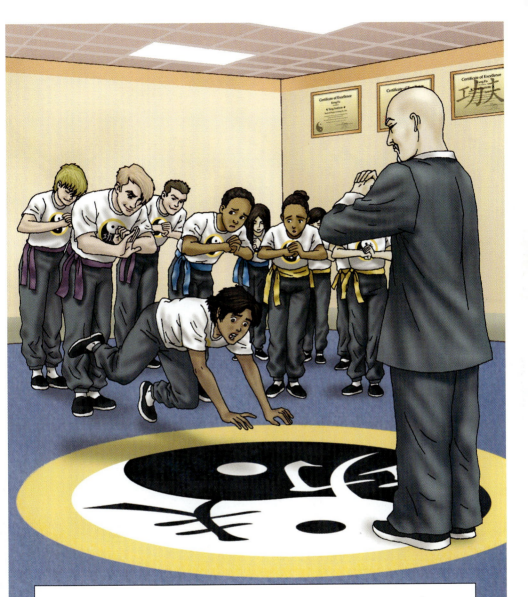

The kung fu teacher bows to the students. The students bow to the teacher.
Scott pushes Adib. The teacher sees Scott push Adib.
Adib falls down in front of the teacher. Everyone is very surprised.
Mike and Scott laugh. But the teacher is not laughing.

The teacher says to Adib, "You're a new student. What's your name?" he asks.

"Adib Murad," he replies.

The teacher says, "Do you know kung fu, Adib?"

"A little," says Adib. "But I want to learn more."

"Okay, Adib," says the teacher. "But first I want to see your kung fu."

The teacher looks at the class.

"Who wants to fight Adib?" he asks.

"I will fight him," says a boy. It is Scott's friend, Mike. Mike is bigger and stronger than Adib.

Mike looks down at Adib. Mike wants to hurt him.

"Okay Mike, you can fight him," says the teacher.

The teacher says, "Let's start. It's a one-minute fight. But don't hit."
The fight starts. Mike tries to kick Adib, but Adib is too fast. He stops the kick, and Mike falls down. Adib is small, but he is very good at kung fu. Everybody is very surprised.

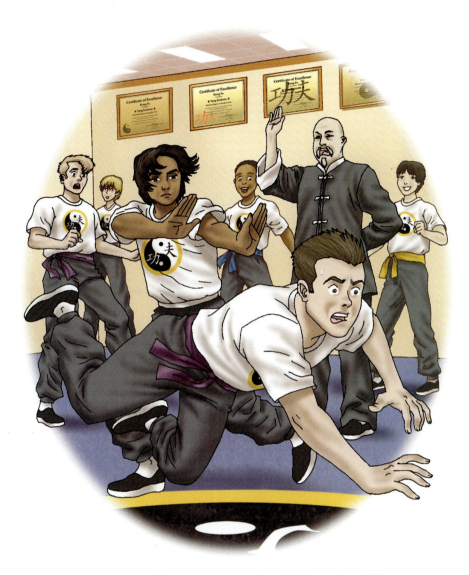

"I'm sorry," says Adib. "Are you okay?" he asks Mike.
But Mike gets up. He is very angry, and he wants to hurt Adib.
"Stop!" says the teacher. "Don't fight!"
But Mike does not listen. He tries to hit Adib in the face, but Adib is too fast.
Adib stops Mike's arm. He pushes Mike in the back, and he falls again.
Scott watches Adib.

"You are very good, Adib," says the teacher. "You don't
hurt people. Very good."
"Umm. . . , thank you, but I want you to teach me
more," says Adib.
The teacher says, "Let's see you fight with our number
one student. Scott, please come here."
Scott comes to Adib. He looks worried!

Scott says, "I'm sorry, my leg hurts today."

"Really, Scott?" says the teacher. He doesn't think Scott is hurt. The teacher says, "Scott, do you want to go home, or fight Adib?"

"Umm. . . , I want to fight," he says. Scott knows Adib is good at kung fu.

"So, please fight Adib. But do not hit," says the teacher. Some of the students start laughing at Scott because he is worried.

Scott looks at Adib. Adib looks at Scott. Scott is taller than Adib, and he is stronger, too.

"Are you ready, little boy?" asks Scott.

"Yes," Adib says. "I'm ready. And I'm not a little boy!"

"Wait. Don't start," says the teacher.

But Scott does not listen. He runs and jumps at Adib.

He tries to kick Adib. Adib is faster than Scott. He moves away, and Scott falls down.

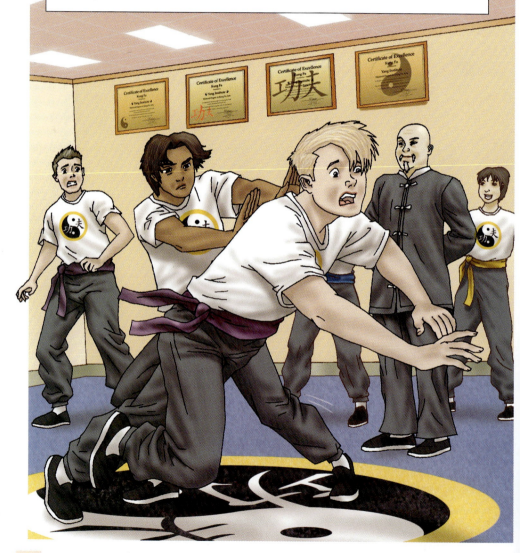

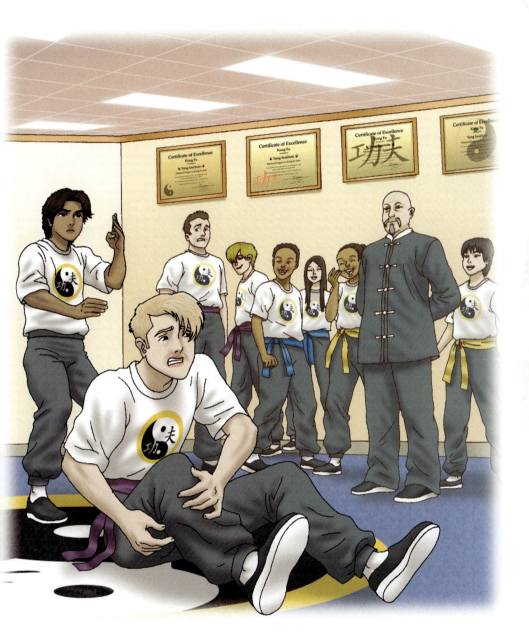

Scott knows Adib is very good. He cannot hit Adib. Adib is too good. Scott is sitting on the floor. He doesn't want to fight Adib now.

He says, "*Ouch*! My leg. I can't fight now. I'm hurt."

Everybody is surprised. They know he is not hurt.

Scott goes out of the room. Everybody knows he is not hurt.
They laugh at him because he does not want to fight Adib.
"Very good, Adib," says the teacher. "You are smaller than
Scott, but you are faster. You are good at kung fu."
"Thank you," Adib replies.
The teacher says, "You are a good student, and a good
teacher, too."

A Good Friend

Written by
Rob Waring and **Maurice Jamall**

Before You Read

to carry

to cut

beach

bottle

foot

forest

guitar

hospital

hurt

jacket

sun

surprised

worried

In the story

Eric

Yoko

Mrs. Ogawa

"Do you want to come?" asks Eric. Eric is at his friend Yoko's house. He and Yoko often go to the beach.
"I'm going down to the beach again. I want to watch the sun go down and sing some songs. We'll have a great time," he says.
"Can you come?" he asks.
"Thanks, Eric. Yeah, I want to come," she says. "I'll ask my mom." She's very excited.

Yoko talks to her mother about Eric.

"Can I go?" Yoko asks her mother.

Mrs. Ogawa looks at Eric. She says, "No. I don't like him. His hair is too long. I don't like that kind of boy. And you are too young for a boyfriend."

"But Mom, he's *not* my boyfriend," says Yoko. "Eric is really nice! It'll be okay, Mom. Please!"

"No!" Mrs. Ogawa says. "No, you can't go out! You have a test tomorrow."

Yoko talks to Eric. "I'm sorry, Eric. I can't go. I have a test tomorrow. Mom wants me to study," she says.
Eric understands. "Oh, I see," he says.
Yoko says, "I'm really sorry, Eric. I really want to come with you."
Eric says, "It's okay. I'll see you at school tomorrow. Bye."
"Yeah. Bye," says Yoko.

Later, Yoko goes back to her room. Yoko doesn't want to study. She wants to be with Eric on the beach.
"I want to see the sun go down," she thinks. "And sing some songs, too."
Yoko thinks about Eric for a long time.
She thinks, "I'm going to see Eric."

Yoko does not tell her mother she wants to go to the beach.
"Mom," she says. "I don't want dinner tonight. I want to study
for tomorrow's test, and then go to sleep," she says.
Yoko's mother is very surprised. "You never study for tests, and
it's only 6 o'clock," she says.
Yoko says, "Good night!"
"Oh, okay. Good night, Yoko," says her mother.
Yoko goes back to her room. But she does not study. She goes
out of her window. She wants to see Eric!

Yoko rides to the beach on her bike.

"Hi, Eric," she says. Yoko smiles at him.

"Yoko!" he says. He is very surprised. "Why are you here?"

Yoko tells him about her mother, and about her lie.

Eric says, "That's not good, Yoko."

"I know," says Yoko. "But I want to see the sun go down with you, Eric."

Eric says, "Your mother will be worried. I'm taking you back home now."

"No, Eric," says Yoko. "I want to sing some songs."
Eric takes her back to her bike. He does not listen to her.
Yoko then says, "Ouch!"
"What's wrong, Yoko?" Eric asks.
"My foot hurts," she says. "The bottle cut my foot."
Eric looks at the bottle. He says, "Oh, no! Are you okay?"
"No, I can't walk," she says.

Yoko cannot ride her bike. They do not have a phone. They cannot call for help. Nobody can help them.

"Yoko, I'll help you get home," says Eric.

Yoko replies, "But what about the bikes, and your guitar?"

"Let's leave the bikes and guitar here," he says. "I'll get them tomorrow."

Eric helps Yoko. She is heavy and it is hard work.

"Eric, I'm sorry," she says. "I can't walk any more. My foot hurts."

Eric carries Yoko a long way. The sun is going down.

Eric says, "I can't go for help and leave you here. I want to take you to the hospital," he says. "Let's keep walking."

"Thanks Eric," she says. "I'm really sorry."

"It's very dark," says Yoko. "I can't see."

"Don't worry, Yoko. I'll help you," says Eric.

Eric says, "Yoko, here, you can have my jacket. You're cold," he says.

He gives Yoko his jacket. "Thanks, Eric," she says. "You're so kind. And you're a good friend."

Then it starts to rain. They start walking again.

It is now 10:30. Yoko's mother goes to Yoko's room to say goodnight. But Yoko is not there. She is not in bed. Mrs. Ogawa looks all over the house.

"Oh no!" thinks Mrs. Ogawa. "Where's Yoko?" She is very worried.

Then she hears the phone. It's Eric.

"Hello, Mrs. Ogawa. This is Eric," he says. "I'm at the hospital with Yoko. Please come."

Mrs. Ogawa goes to the hospital.

Mrs. Ogawa is very happy to see Yoko again.
"Yoko, are you okay?" she asks.
"I'm fine now, but my foot hurts," she says. "Mom, I'm really sorry."
"That's okay," her mother says. "You are okay now."
Mrs. Ogawa thinks Eric is bad because Yoko is hurt. She does not know about Yoko's lie. She does not know about Eric's help.
"Eric, I'm really angry with you. Don't ask Yoko to go to the beach again," she says.

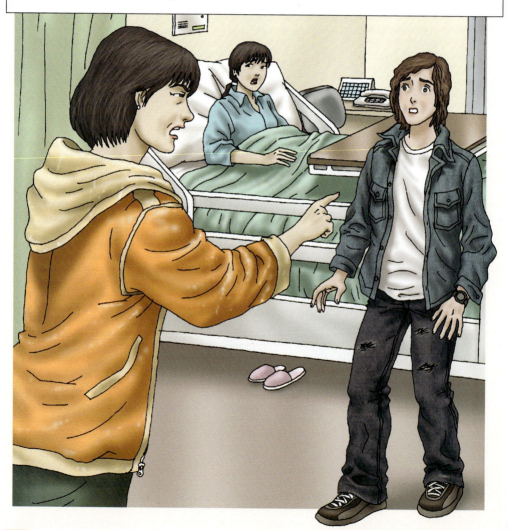

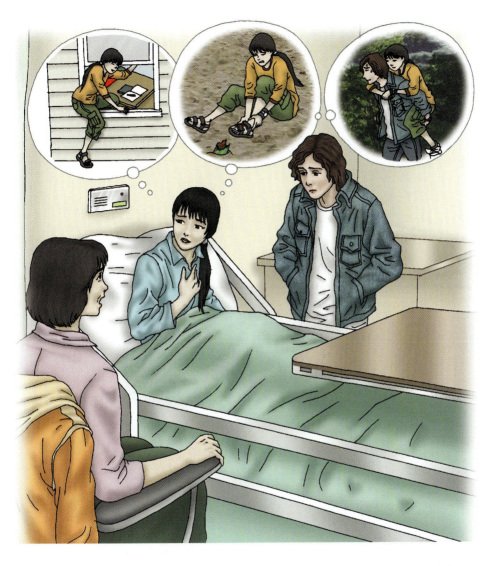

Yoko says, "But, Mom, Eric is not the bad one. I'm the bad one."
"Why?" Mrs. Ogawa asks. "Tell me about tonight, Yoko. I want to know everything!"
Yoko tells her Mom about the lie, the bottle, and about Eric's help.
"Oh, I see," she says. "Well, thank you, Eric. I'm sorry, Eric. You are a good friend to Yoko."

Yoko's mother goes home.

"I'm going home now," says Eric. "My parents will be worried. I'll come and see you tomorrow after the test."

Yoko says, "Thanks again, Eric. You're a good friend."

"That's okay," he replies.

He looks at her and smiles. He says, "You are more than a good friend to me."

Quick Thinking

Written by
Rob Waring and **Maurice Jamall**

Before You Read

to drop

to fall

to fly

to swim

beach

car

a cart

lake

plane

police officer

quick

In the story

Faye

David

Tyler

Daniela

John

John and Tyler are in the park. They are showing everybody their cars and planes.
"These are really great!" says Tyler. John talks to his friends Faye and David.
"Faye and David, do you want to try?" asks John.
Faye says, "No thanks, we're going to the beach."
"Do you want to come?" asks David.

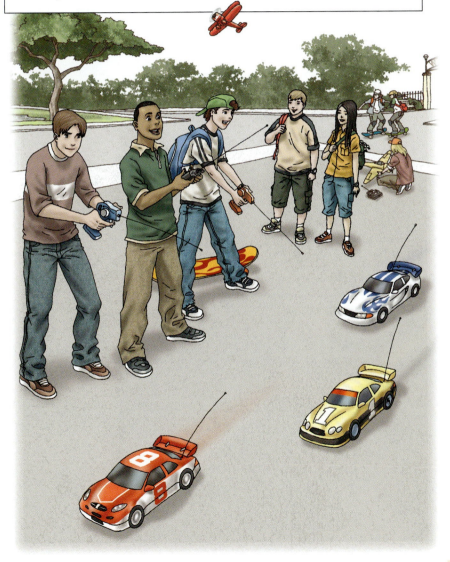

"No thanks, David," John says. "Have a good time at the beach."

"Okay, see you later," say David and Faye.

David says, "It's a great day to swim. Come on, Faye."

"Yes, let's go," replies Faye.

John and Tyler play with their cars and planes in the park.

David and Faye go down to the beach. They see their friend Daniela.

"Hi, Daniela, it's hot today!" says Faye.

"Hi. Yeah. Do you want ice cream?" Daniela asks.

Faye says, "Yes, please." David gives her the money.

"We're going swimming," says Faye.

"Okay, have a good time. See you later," says Daniela.

Faye and David walk down onto the beach. They are going swimming.
There are many people on the beach. Some people are walking on the beach. Dogs are playing on the beach, too. Everybody is having a great time.

Faye and David put their things on the beach.
They are getting ready to swim.
They see a man running on the beach.
"David, what's that man doing?" asks Faye.
"I don't know," replies David. "I don't know."
"He's running very fast," says Faye.

The man has a bag.

"Stop! Stop!" shouts a woman. "Stop him! He has my bag."

Faye says, "That man has the woman's bag!"

"Quick, let's stop him," says David.

"But how? Think. Quick, David, think!" says Faye.

The man is running away.

"Where's he going?" asks David.

"He's going to the street, I think," Faye says.

Faye gets her phone. She calls Daniela.

"Daniela, it's Faye. Stop that man, Daniela," she says.

"Okay, but which man?" asks Daniela.

"The man in gray. He has a woman's bag. He's coming to you," says Faye.

"Okay, I can see him," says Daniela. "I'll stop him," she says.

Daniela pushes the cart into the man. The man falls down. He drops the woman's bag.
Daniela tries to stop the man, but she can't. The man is very big and he's too strong. Daniela can't stop him.
The man gets up and takes the woman's bag. He runs away to the park.

Faye and David run to Daniela.

"Are you okay, Daniela?" they ask.

"Yes, I'm okay," she says. "I'm sorry, he's running away.
He's going into the park."

Daniela says, "Let's stop him."

"But how?" asks Faye. "What can we do, David?" she asks.
"Do you have an idea?"

David calls Tyler.

"Tyler, it's David," he says. "Can you see a man running into the park?"

Tyler asks, "Yes. Does he have gray pants and a gray shirt?"

"Yes," says David. "Stop him! He has a woman's bag."

"Okay, we'll stop him. But how?" asks Tyler. "He's a big man. I can't stop him."

"Think!" says David.

Tyler tells John about the man. The man is running
through the park with the woman's bag.
"He's running very fast," says John.
Tyler asks, "How can we stop him? He's running too fast."
"I have an idea," says John. "I know! We can stop him!"

"Let's use the cars and planes," says John. John makes his car go to the man. John's car hits the man.
"Good job, John!" says Tyler. Tyler's car hits the man, too. The man is surprised and he falls over. He drops the bag. Tyler and John tell the other boys about the man.

Many people help John and Tyler. They want to
stop the man. Their cars and planes fly at the man.
Tyler's car hits the man again and again. This time,
the man falls into the lake.
"Good job, Tyler!" says John.

The man is under the tree. He cannot run away. He is wet and cold. Two police officers come to the park.

"Thank you, thank you very much," says a police officer.

Tyler tells him about Faye, David and Daniela, too.

"That *is* quick thinking!" he says.

I Always Win!

Written by
Rob Waring and **Maurice Jamall**

to remember

a race

to win

starting line

corner

trees

cup

fast

finish line

gate

second, first, third

Tyler   Ryan   Mr. Walsh

"Are you ready, Tyler?" asks his friend, Eric.
"Yes, I'm ready," Tyler replies.
Today is a big day in Bayview. There is a big bike race today. Everybody is very excited. Ryan is in the race, too. Tyler and Ryan are both very good riders. They both want to win the race.

Tyler's friends John, and Eric want him to win.
"Have a good race, Tyler," says Eric.
"Thanks, I want to win this year," says Tyler.
John says, "Ryan wins every year. But I think you'll win today."
"Be careful of Ryan. He's very fast," says Eric.
"I know," Tyler replies. "I'll watch him."

Ryan is with his father, Mr. Walsh. Ryan has a new bike.
Every year Ryan's father buys him a new bike for this race.
It is a very good bike. It is very fast. Ryan is very happy.
"I'll win this race again this year, too, with my new bike,"
Ryan thinks.

Ryan's father is talking to Ryan.
"I want you to win. Our family always finishes first,"
Mr. Walsh says. "We always win. Do you understand?"
"Yes, Dad," says Ryan. "I understand. Our family
always wins."
His father says, "I want you to go faster than last year,
okay? You *will* win today. Okay?"
Ryan is worried but he says, "Yes, Dad."

Tyler, Ryan, and the other riders go to the starting line.
Ryan is worried about the race. He looks at his father.
His father really wants Ryan to win. Ryan looks at Tyler.
He knows Tyler wants to win, too.
"I'll win today. I'm Ryan Walsh! I always win," Ryan thinks.
"I have a good bike and I'm a good rider. I'm very good,"
he thinks.

Tyler looks at Ryan's new bike. "Is that a new bike, Ryan?" he asks.

"Yes," Ryan says. "Do you like it?"

Tyler says, "You have a good bike, but I'm going to win. Let's have a good race."

"Yeah," Ryan replies. "I'll see you at the finish line."

Tyler and Ryan start very fast. They are winning.
They are faster than the other riders. They go faster
and faster. Tyler and Ryan race around a corner.
"Good, I'm winning," thinks Tyler.
Ryan is second but he is going fast, too.

They go up and down. They go through the trees.
They go through a river. It is a very good race.
Tyler is going fast and Ryan is going fast, too.
Now Ryan is winning. And Tyler is second.

Go
Tyler!

03

02

They race through some more trees. Tyler and Ryan are tired, but they both want to win today. "I always win!" thinks Ryan. "I can't be second! I won't be second!"

"I'll win today!" thinks Tyler.

They go faster and faster. It is a great race.

They see a gate. They race to it. The first person to the gate will win the race. The two bikes are very close. Ryan goes faster, but Tyler is winning.

"I want to be first to the gate," thinks Ryan. "I want to win! I always win!"

Tyler is winning, but Ryan wants to get to the gate first. He goes faster than Tyler.
Ryan thinks about his father's words. "We always win!" he remembers. "We always win!"
Tyler sees Ryan's bike getting closer and closer.

Ryan does not want Tyler to win. Ryan pushes Tyler.
Tyler shouts, "Hey! What are you doing?"
Tyler's bike hits the gate. He falls off his bike. Ryan goes
through the gate. Ryan goes on to the finish line. He wins
the race.

Ryan gets the cup. His father is very happy.
"Good job, Ryan," says his father.
Ryan says nothing. He is not happy.
Tyler looks at Ryan. Ryan looks at Tyler.
"Umm. . . Dad?. . . ," Ryan says. "I want to tell
you something. . ."

Later that day, Ryan and his father go to see Tyler.
"This is your cup, not mine," says Ryan. He gives
Tyler the cup.
"I'm really sorry," Ryan says. Tyler smiles.
"Are you okay?" asks Ryan.
"Thanks, Ryan," says Tyler. "I'm okay now."

Quiz Night

Written by
Rob Waring and **Maurice Jamall**

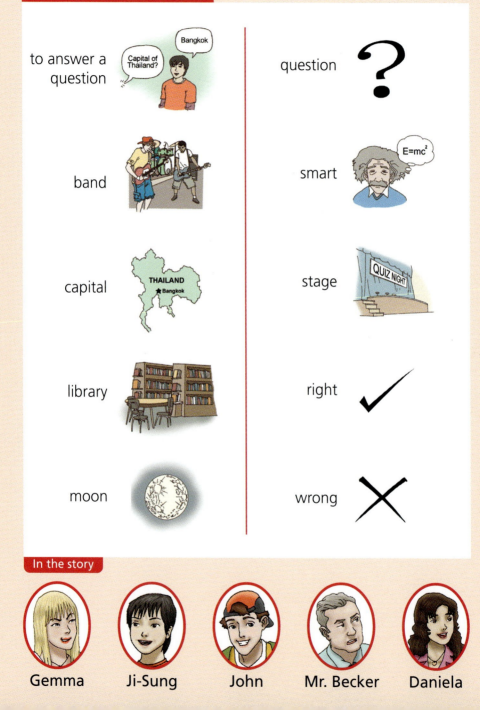

to answer a question

question

band

smart

capital

stage

library

right

moon

wrong

In the story

Gemma

Ji-Sung

John

Mr. Becker

Daniela

"There's a Quiz Night, next Saturday," says Daniela.
Ji-Sung, John, and Daniela are looking at a poster.
"Ji-Sung, are you going to be in the Quiz Night? You're
very smart," says John.
Daniela says, "Yes, you can win some pizza tickets, too."
"Yes, I think I'll go," says Ji-Sung. "I can win. And then
I'll give you some pizza."
"Wow, thanks," says John. "I *love* pizza!"

Daniela asks, "John, are you in the Quiz Night?"
"No, I'm helping with the questions," he says. "Mr. Becker and I are making the questions for the Quiz Night. We're going to the library tomorrow afternoon," he says.
"Wow, that's great, John," says Daniela. "Don't make the questions too difficult!"
A girl is watching them. Her name is Gemma.

The next day, Mr. Becker and John are in the library. They are making questions for the Quiz Night. Gemma comes to them. She knows they are making the questions.

"What are you doing?" she asks.

Gemma tries to look at the questions. But Mr. Becker puts his paper under a book.

"We are making questions for the Quiz Night. Please don't look," says Mr. Becker.

"Oh, sorry," she says.

Later Gemma sees John. She asks, "John, do you want some money?"

"No. Why?" asks John.

"Give me the questions and answers for the quiz," says Gemma.

John is very surprised. "No, I will *not* give you the answers. Go away!" says John.

"Come on, John. It's okay, nobody will know," says Gemma.

"No! No! And no again!" says John. He's angry with Gemma. He doesn't like her.

It is Saturday, and it is Quiz Night. There are six people. They all want to win.

Mr. Becker says, "Let's start. All the players will answer some questions. One wrong answer and you are out. Do you understand?" he says. Everybody understands.

John gets the first ball.

"The first question is for Yoon-Hee," says Mr. Becker. A tall girl answers the first question. Yoon-Hee is Ji-Sung's sister.

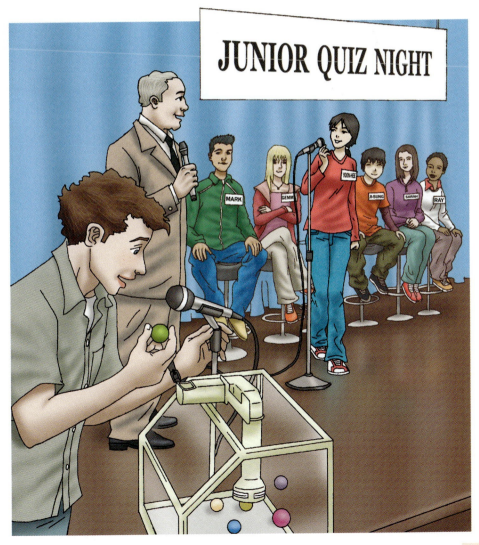

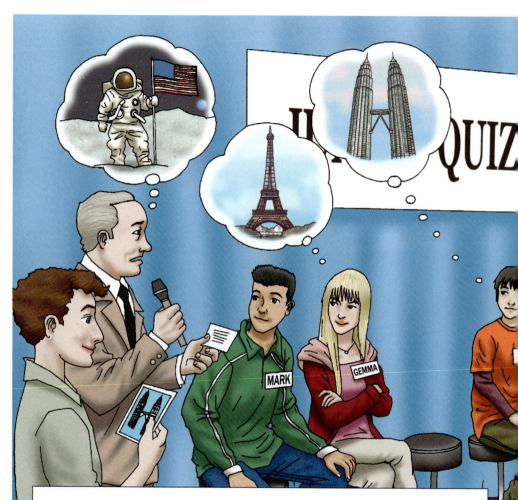

"Yoon-Hee, what's the name of the first man on the moon?" Mr. Becker asks.

Yoon-Hee answers, "Yuri Gagarin."

"No, I'm sorry, Yoon-Hee, that's the wrong answer," says Mr. Becker. "It's Neil Armstrong. You are out."

"Sarah, what's the name of the writer of the *Harry Potter* books?" he asks.

She answers, "I don't know. Is it Anita Rodling?"

"No, I'm sorry, it's not. It's J.K. Rowling. Sorry, you're out, too," says Mr. Becker.

Mr. Becker asks Gemma the next question.
"Gemma, what's the name of the tall tower in Paris?"
"It's the Eiffel Tower," she says.
Mr. Becker says, "That's right!"
"The next question is for Ji-Sung. Ji-Sung, where are the Petronas Towers?" he asks.
Ji-Sung answers, "They're in Kuala Lumpur, in Malaysia."
"That's right!" says Mr. Becker.

Mr. Becker asks Ji-Sung the next question.

"Which British rock band sings the song *Yesterday*, Ji-Sung?

"Is it The Beatles?" answers Ji-Sung.

Mr. Becker says, "That's right. Okay. Now, the next question."

"Mark, the White House is in the United States. Where's the Blue House?" asks Mr. Becker.

"Is it in India?" asks Mark.

"No, I'm sorry it's not. It's in South Korea. I'm sorry, you're out," says Mr. Becker.

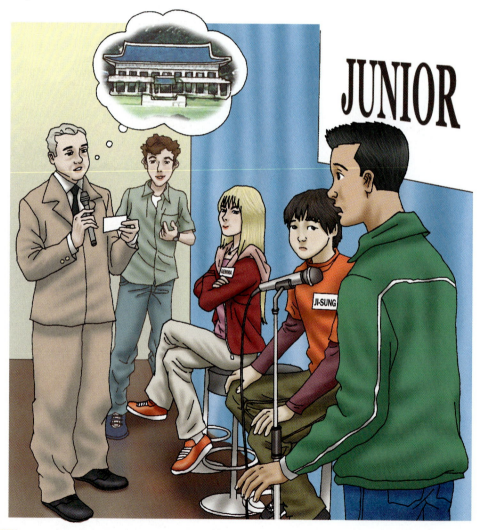

Gemma and Ji-Sung are very good. They get all their
questions right.
"Gemma, what's the capital of Vietnam?" asks Mr. Becker.
"It's Hanoi," says Gemma.
Mr. Becker says, "That's right!"
"Ji-Sung, which two languages do people speak in
Canada?" he asks.
"English and French," Ji-Sung says.
"Very good!" says Mr. Becker.

John talks to everybody. He says, "Well, there are only two people, Gemma and Ji-Sung. Who will win?" he asks.
He says, "We'll now listen to some music. We'll start the questions again in ten minutes."
Ji-Sung and Gemma go to their friends. John does not want Gemma to win. He wants to help Ji-Sung. John comes to talk to Ji-Sung.

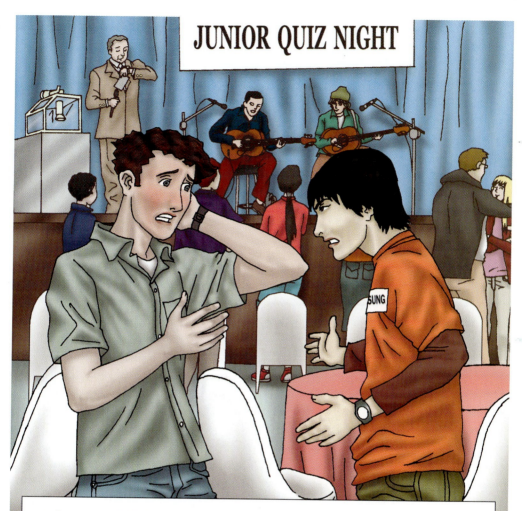

John says, "Ji-Sung, what's the capital of Thailand?"

"It's Bangkok," Ji-Sung answers. "Why do you ask?" he asks.

"Oh, you know that!" says John. "It's okay."

Ji-Sung asks, "John, why are you asking?"

"It's the next question," John replies.

"What? It's the next question? Oh no!" he says. "I can't win now!"

"But, you know the answer . . . ," says John.

"Yes, but I know the question!" Ji-Sung says. He is very angry with John.

Ji-Sung goes back to the stage. He is looking at John. He is very angry with him. He is waiting for his question.

Mr. Becker asks, "Ji-Sung, what's the capital of Thailand?"

Ji-Sung looks at John and says, "I don't know!"

John is very surprised. "What's Ji-Sung doing?" he thinks. "He knows the answer! I don't understand."

Mr. Becker asks, "Gemma, what's the capital of Thailand?"

"Bangkok!" she says.

"Gemma's the winner!" says Mr. Becker. "Congratulations!"

Ji-Sung goes back to his friends. He is very angry with John.
"It's okay," says Mark.
"Bad luck," says Daniela.
"That's okay," says Ji-Sung. "I can't win everything! What do *you* think, John?" he asks.
"Yes, you're right," John says. John puts his head down and everyone looks at him. His face is very red.

"Let's all go and get some pizza," says Daniela.
Yoon-Hee says, "Okay, good idea! Let's go everybody."
"Umm. . . , I'm not coming," says John. Everybody looks at John.
They are surprised.
"But you love pizza, John!" says Daniela.
John looks at Ji-Sung. "I'm not hungry now," he says.

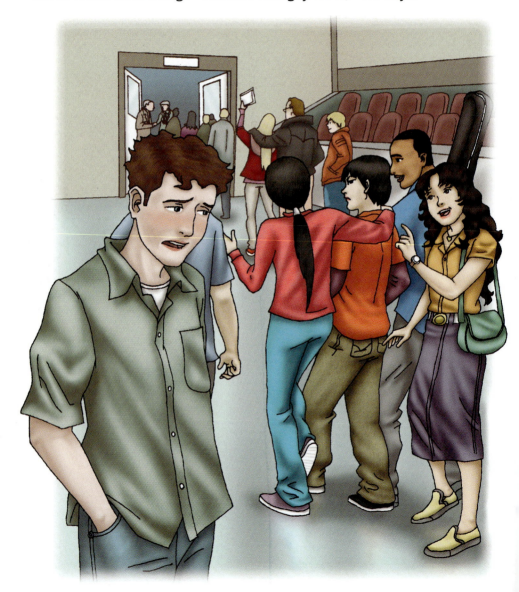